D1061439

TOOLS FOR TEACHERS

- **ATOS:** 0.9
- **GRL:** C
- **WORD COUNT:** 68
- **CURRICULUM CONNECTIONS:** animals, habitats

Skills to Teach

- **HIGH-FREQUENCY WORDS:** full, in, is, of, the, there, too, who
- **CONTENT WORDS:** corals, dolphins, fish, jellyfish, life, ocean, seals, sea stars, sea turtles, sharks, squids, whales
- **PUNCTUATION:** periods, commas, exclamation points, question mark
- **WORD STUDY:** schwa /ə/ (*corals*, *ocean*); /sh/, spelled *c* (*ocean*); /f/, spelled *ph* (*dolphins*); multisyllable words (*corals*, *dolphins*, *jellyfish*, *ocean*, *turtles*)
- **TEXT TYPE:** information report

Before Reading Activities

- Read the title and give a simple statement of the main idea.
- Have students "walk" though the book and talk about what they see in the pictures.
- Introduce new vocabulary by having students predict the first letter and locate the word in the text.
- Discuss any unfamiliar concepts that are in the text.

After Reading Activities

The book's text tells us that each animal lives in the ocean, but the photos can be used to gather extra information. Encourage children to talk about the different things animals are shown doing in the book. What other words could they use in place of "live" or "in the ocean"? For example, "Whales jump in the ocean," "Fish swim in the ocean," or even "Seals rest on a rock."

Tadpole Books are published by Jump!, 5357 Penn Avenue South, Minneapolis, MN 55419, www.jumplibrary.com

Editorial: Hundred Acre Words, LLC **Designer:** Anna Peterson

Photo Credits: Deposit Photos: GoodOlga, 12–13. Getty: danilovi, 14–15; Georgette Douwma, 2–3. iStock: mbolina, 10–11. National Geographic: DAVID LIITSCHWAGER, 6–7. Nature Picture Library: Alex Mustard, 4–5. Shutterstock: Andrea Izzotti, 8–9; bluehand, cover, 6–7; Dancestrokes, 12–13; itor, 1; Max Topchii, 14–15; Potapov Alexander, cover; Tory Kallman, 12–13; tubuceo, 4–5

Library of Congress Cataloging-in-Publication Data
Names: Fretland VanVoorst, Jenny, 1972– author.
Title: Who lives in the ocean? / by Jenny Fretland VanVoorst.
Description: Minneapolis, MN: Jump!, Inc., (2017) | Series: Who lives here? | Audience: Ages 3–6. | Includes index.
Identifiers: LCCN 2017023539 (print) | LCCN 2017022496 (ebook) | ISBN 9781624967276 (ebook) | ISBN 9781620319574 (hardcover: alk. paper) | ISBN 9781620319581 (pbk.)
Subjects: LCSH: Marine animals—Juvenile literature.
Classification: LCC QL122.2 (print) | LCC QL122.2 F76 2017 (ebook) | DDC 591.77—dc23
LC record available at https://lccn.loc.gov/2017023539

WHO LIVES HERE?

WHO LIVES IN THE OCEAN?

by Jenny Fretland VanVoorst

TABLE OF CONTENTS

WHO LIVES IN THE OCEAN?

The ocean is full of life.

Who lives there?

Sharks live in the ocean.

Coral lives there, too.

Fish live in the ocean.

Squid live there, too.

Sea stars live in the ocean.

Dolphins live there, too.

Sea turtles live in the ocean.

Jellyfish live there, too.

Seals live in the ocean.

Whales live there, too.

Wow!

The ocean
is full of life!

WORDS TO KNOW

coral

dolphin

fish

seal

sea turtle

whale

INDEX